Fort Red Border

FORT
RED
BORDER

POEMS
Kiki
Petrosino

Sarabande Books
LOUISVILLE, KENTUCKY

Managing Editor
Sarabande Books, Inc.
2234 Dundee Road, Suite 200
Louisville, KY 40205

Library of Congress Cataloging-in-Publication Data

Petrosino, Kiki, 1979–
    Fort red border : poems / by Kiki Petrosino. — 1st ed.
        p.   cm.
    ISBN 978-1-932511-74-1 (pbk. : acid-free paper)
    I. Title.
    PS3616.E868F67 2009
    811'.6—dc22   2008041310
ISBN-13: 978-1-932511-74-1

Cover photograph by Philip Miller

Manufactured in Canada
This book is printed on acid-free paper.

Sarabande Books is a nonprofit literary organization.

NATIONAL
ENDOWMENT
FOR THE ARTS

This project is supported in part by an award from the National
Endowment for the Arts.

KENTUCKY
Arts
COUNCIL

The Kentucky Arts Council, a state agency in the Commerce
Cabinet, provides operational support funding for Sarabande
Books with state tax dollars and federal funding from the National
Endowment for the Arts, which believes that a great nation
deserves great art.

For my family & for Philip

CONTENTS

ACKNOWLEDGMENTS

Many thanks to the editors of the following publications where versions of these poems first appeared:

Shifter: "Coffee," "China Clipper," "Sonnet K," "Bitchfoxly"; *Fence Magazine*: "This Will Darken the Cabin," "Dread," "Nestlé"; *Harvard Review*: "Afro"; *McSweeneys.net*: "Crusaders"; *42opus*: "You Have Made a Career of Not Listening"; *Forklift, Ohio*: "Anecdote," "Secret Ninja"; *Alimentum*: "Gristle," "Valentine [I hope your father]"; *Born Magazine*: "I didn't know infants in arms until"; *La Petite Zine*: "O Lord"; *Siren*: "When My Afro is White with Dotage," "Crossing"; *POOL*: "Valentine [Maybe you were]"; *Dragonfire*: "Valentine [Today I met]"; *Unpleasant Event Schedule*: "Valentine [In Chicago]," "Valentine [I build you]"; *The Iowa Review*: "Valentine [Sorry, but]," "Valentine [Today I got rejected]"

"You Have Made a Career of Not Listening" was printed in *Best New Poets 2006* (Samovar Press, 2006). "Saints" and "Valentine [Once I was]" were recorded and archived as a video reading for *The Continental Review* (November 2007). Some lines that became the poem "Afro" appeared at the University of Iowa as a broadside designed by Ben Estes and Tammy Petro and printed at the UI Centre for the Book (Winter 2008). "White" appeared at the University of Cincinnati Moor Poetry Reading Series as a broadside designed by Evan Commander (April 2008).

I'm grateful to the University of Chicago, the University of Iowa (especially the Iowa Writers' Workshop and the International Writing Program), the Bread Loaf Writers' Conference, and the Rolex Mentor and Protégé Arts Initiative for their support and recognition of this work. For inspiration, a job, and vocabulary words, thanks to Dr. Richard Smith of *The Annals of Otology, Rhinology, and Laryngology*. For guidance, friendship, and encouragement, my gratitude to Srikanth Reddy, Christopher Merrill, Eavan Boland, Michael Collier, Dean Young, Mark Levine, James Galvin, Cole Swensen, Marvin Bell, Lan Samantha Chang, Connie Brothers, Rebecca Wolff, D.A. Powell, James Longenbach, Major Jackson, Hugh Ferrer, Nataša Ďurovičová, Matt Hart, Steve Grant, Zach Savich, Leslie Jamison, Edan Lepucki, Madeline McDonnell, Carol Quinn, Julia Whicker Schoolmeester, Dina Hardy, Kristin Hatch, Kaethe Schwehn, Nico Alvarado-Greenwood, Mia Nussbaum, Dan Kennedy, Kim Brooks, Joe McPherson, Patrick McIntosh, Rob Thornett, Norah Smith, Chris Chesley, and Bill Gelfeld.

—a thing like me,
but not the thing I asked for, a thing by accident or
design, I am now attached to.

—Brigit Pegeen Kelly

Fort Red Border

WASH

So I lean back & Redford asks, "Water warm enough?"
& I don't answer because I'm holding my breath.
I don't know why he asks.
He never uses the faucet to shampoo my afro—just an old clay jar.
Redford fills the jar at the backyard pump.
Then he leaves it in the sun to heat.
So it's only going to be so warm by the time it gets to me.
That's the point of doing things natural:
You get what the sun dishes out, not what you customize.
The sun is not a customizable thing.
I try to say this.
Redford leans over me with his hands full of shampoo.
His blue shirt skims my face.
There is a dark hole in the armpit.
If it were a wound, it would be terrible.
I glimpse the long curve of Redford's body through the hole.
There's his arm, stretched above me.
Then a smooth triangle of torso disappearing into shadows.
His shadows are grey & brown as grass.
There's no sun here.
But some lights are moving—tea-colored, delicate.
The pale ribs move in Redford's flank.
It's these that help him breathe.
Ribs have their own set of shadows, their own lights.
I count the shadows, then.
I count the lights.

COFFEE

Redford & I are having coffee together.
It's 6 a.m.—I've tied my afro in the pale green scarf
he brought me years ago from Malta. It took us
fifteen minutes to get here. We're standing just above
the treeline, at the white crest of a window, in a tower room paved
with blistering planks. *I've never been to Malta. Does it snow*
much there? I pour the coffee from my best thermos, the one
with the French press inside. The brimless metal cup shifts
in Redford's hand. *Terribly,* he says & moves
his other hand to the tender of my back. *Drifts so high, you can't*
waltz through. I imagine us there, in yellow opera cloaks
& Maltese snowshoes, back-step-turning beneath the shadowy
ice towers. I lean back & Redford traces my spine
with his thumb. I feel as though I've just done well on something—
my Algebra exam, the fragile zipper on my tightest
dress, my federal taxes. *Let me get you something*
now. His wide palm disappears from my skin, leaving a hard
flag of heat. From his leather satchel, Redford lifts
two heavy slices of baguette spread liberally
with chèvre & wrapped in wax paper. *Just a second, don't*
eat that yet. He tilts the bread in my hand. Adds a crinkle
of fresh rucola. *There.* We watch the broken polo fields fill up
with fog. I tell Redford how, after saving Peter
the Never Bird slips away from their island, sheltering
her eggs in the top hat Peter gave her. The top hat is silk
& black with a plain brim. The top hat is 100% waterproof.

How fine, Redford says. His tanned face is very still. In the shallows of his ears, the new sun reddens & I look away from him then in the direction of roofs.

THIS WILL DARKEN THE CABIN

Halfway through my plate of tiger prawns
Redford returns from the cockpit tour.
Such a face, he says. *Were you this soulful as a child?*
He tips my chin & slides my headset back.
I've been listening to the pilots marking weather
in their code talk. Right now we're at two-five-five
knots, heading straight into the soup above
Las Vegas. Our pilot has a clean, grey voice—
like creosote or silverware. He's just said *advise*.
He's just said *preparing*. Redford eases
into his seat, folding one knee
over the other. He rolls his double brandy
in a plastic snifter. The cuffs of his soft green shirt
are pushed into his elbows. *I had some soulful ways, I guess.*
I tuck into a small ramekin of green gage plums
soaked in cream & rice vinegar. At the edge
of my vision, Redford lifts his spoon, considering
the loose pyramid of Asian jungle fowl
on his tray. I pick up a tiny package
of salt. *Know what I used to do with this?*
I reach across Redford's lap, taking a lengthy swallow
of brandy from his glass. *At night, I'd eat this.*
It was a thing. I'd pour a whole bunch
in my mouth & then I'd chew until my tongue opened.
For the first time, I notice how it's very quiet
here in First Class. I drain the brandy, listening to the *hum hum*
of the cabin lights against my gulps. Below us, Las Vegas

is an orange watch glass someone shattered. I think
about the neon people down there, the funny cowboy with tubes
of brown light for a ten-gallon hat, & I think how hard it must be
to make brown neon, & how we still need science.
After a moment, I feel Redford take the snifter
from my hand. He lowers it into the circular depression
in his tray. The plastic hazes where my palm
has touched. Redford reaches over, snapping
my tray into the seatback. Then he finds the place
where my safety belt catches. He gently pulls until
the belt tightens, low & quiet on my hips. He keeps his palm
on the buckle & I settle back. What made me, made me.
Above our heads the reading lights go out.

CANTO THIRTEEN

I wake up crying. There's no sound, just my throat
pushing hard into the mattress. When I turn to check
the alarm clock, a few tears pull across my neck & through
my nightgown. I drag the sheet away from my collarbone, taking
a long breath that seems to catch in the middle. It's late.
Flakes of radio static collect in my throat. I keep trying
to swallow, & a brown choke of breath slips out.
Hey—Redford reaches up to touch the center
of my back. I look down at him, blinking. I don't know
how long he's been listening there. The sheets
have dropped from the long snowfield of his body. As he reaches
for his glasses on the nightstand, I feel the mattress
give; a slight hollow of warmth opens just under
my knees. Redford sits up & slides one arm
around my waist: I relax into his bare
shoulder. The slender rise of his collarbone makes a ridge
under my cheek, like the worn fish traps they've found in dry
moat beds near the Tower of London, delicate forked machines
of flint & willow, no bigger than a thumbspan, & so thinned
by water they're nearly colorless. Redford brushes
his fingertips over the nape of my neck. He pauses at the tiny curls
that mark my hairline. I close my eyes, listening
to the dark sounds of his breathing. When I was born, my grandmother
held me by the ankles, looking for resemblances
in the orange light above the stove. When she saw my neck, she gave
me back to my mother. *At least she has a kitchen*, she said.
Otherwise, she hardly looks like me. I take a sip of air

then look up at Redford. A watery rope of moonlight tumbles
over his forehead & across his teeth. I lift my hand to his lips & hold
it there. This is the sound of the willow.

DREAD

On a broken day of thundersnows, Redford watches as I gather my afro into a plain elastic hoop. This is how I pull it back: both hands, a ballet circle of turned elbows, my own putting-off crown. *Is this* he asks *how your mother wears it?* He traces a soft cross at my nape. I tilt my head to look at him. *Not even close* I grin. *She doesn't keep it natural.* I take my hands down. Redford's face goes coltish & aware. *Is that how you say it, natural?* In his voice, the word fills up with weather—a pinnace moving slowly through the Chesapeake, sun darkening its wooden planks to blue. I close my eyes, counting back from several. *There isn't any special way to say it.* I'm listening to the spilled needlebox of thunder, to the sodden sweep of passing cars like flair pens over a sheet of pale manila. *Well* Redford says. *I want to know about it* & for a long time, I sit with my hands folded against my knees. We had a metal sink. Every six weeks, my mother brushed a heavy mask of detergents over me. There was straightening lotion. There were courtroom dramas on the television by the stove. There was carrot protein & ginseng & watercress extract. She went in sections, pulling hard with the comb attachment on the hairdryer. It was on Sundays, & the comb wasn't deep enough for our kind of hair. You had to keep pulling, or the heat wouldn't go through. *It wasn't for always* I tell Redford. *If it rained, your hair went back. You couldn't sweat. That's what natural means.* But at night, I would dream yellowly of hands slanting through the walls, or else of horses tearing into long canyons of dashed, bitter grass. Next morning, I felt the old warp at the roots of my hair again, a kind of lifting that lasted & grew deeper. I tell Redford: *I just couldn't keep down.* So that's the beginning.

CRANS MONTANA

I reach out, & Redford hands me a silver tube of mayo. We're sharing *pommes frittes* in the empty restaurant at the top of Bella Lui. In the half-dark under the dinette, our discarded fleeces tangle & steam; new water weeps from the cuffs of our ski pants. We're not going back up the glacier. *Far too brown today* Redford sighs, dipping a fry into the smooth X of mayonnaise on his napkin. *I was skiing over thistles.* It's true; the last snow bridges have melted, leaving rounds of turf large enough to stand in. Redford's not that worried—this is what he calls the *vestibule* of summer ski—but all morning I orbited the lift station, practicing my carving technique on the gentlest slopes I could find. Even then, I kept crossing the tips of my skis & sagging forward, the distance to the ground impossibly long & slow, as in the many dreams of falling—past branches, railings, fences—that blurred my sleep in the high resort bed. From across the colorless glacier I'd see Redford, his ski jacket ablaze with strength, gathering for a jump or swerving into a shallow field of moguls with his poles crooked tightly into his flank. I was exhausted from hating my body, which dangled uselessly above my rented skis, curling itself inward like a raw shrimp. I wanted a million flapjacks & the Eurythmics on the radio by the cash register; the chalky tang of pillow mints & the big honest cutlery of my people. *Stupid Europe. Stupid raclette* I thought, then toppled backward, wrenching my boot from its latch. I heard my left ski click, then watched it float down the embankment, a bright gondola hewn from carbon Kevlar, a-going someplace smooth. *I should go* I thought without moving. *I should go now.* A small clod of snow dropped from my headband, melting into the back of my suede glove. *Op-la!* Redford called from his moguls. There he was, working into a rare drift of them, his face a flat dial beneath the silent funicular cables. I unlatched my other ski, pushed it down to disappear, too, behind a rise. A long time passed without speaking. Now, crumpling the napkin in his fist, Redford asks: *What were you doing out there, with your equipment?* There's nothing to tell him. With my tongue, I draw a secret tiger on the roof of my mouth. Mostly, I am patient.

CHINA CLIPPER

Redford & I are alone in the darkened galley
of the Martin M-130 flying boat that rests on the exhibition floor
of the City Museum of Industry. We don't have much
room—just this narrow strip of tile between two
moulded counters & a miniature drinks trolley
with its wheels glued down. The cabinets above our heads shelter
a permanent supply of gilt-rimmed fiberglass plates
& Kirk Stieff silver welded into bristling
thickets of service. I'm standing so close to Redford
that the chemical taste of his aftershave mingles with the flakes
of dust that peel down from the highball glasses.
Redford presses my hand tightly into his chest. *Darling—*
I could marry you in this goddamned airliner, built or unbuilt.
His mouth tastes warmly of night mail & belted
trenchcoats. On that breakfast approach to Midway
at 150 mph, the Chief Engineer watched gooney birds thicken
& glow above the island & grinned over the hydromatic
rim of his coffee. As for me, I've crossed
the International Dateline & felt
so much older afterward, as if my body had adjourned
into hollow stalks of cane. Many times it was
like that for me, alone. I could move in two
directions at once—it was a broken
kind of trying I could not tell the bottom of.
It stirred with me in rooms, a frightened thing
of glass & shifting wire. I didn't tell about it.
Only held with it & fevered nightwise over slanting

13

countries of my thought—& then there was no
taking back that trying from me, & I was made for being this
& this is how. *This is how*—in the half-dark, Redford, even closer.
I kiss his jaw & say *This is the maiden flight of harm, the green*
air above Manila. I slowly draw his collar open.
I feel his ribcage lift against me: *Tell me what*
thou art, wild. & then: *What art thou, wild?*
The floor begins to sound & tilt; we quicken
in the blackest way of engines.
I tell Redford *I want such days as days forgive.*
I flick my tongue across his bottom lip.
How can I keep from singing?

MUSTANG BAGEL

Even at my favorite coffeeshop downtown, Redford
is a hard man to feed. This morning, he picks
at his Grilled Asiago Mastercrust with a slow, disdainful frown.
Could they spare the fromage on this so-called "treat?"
He takes a sip of hazlenut coffee, then winces delicately
into the neck of his sweater vest. I bite powerfully
through my Cinnamon Frenchroll: *Well, if you really don't think*
you got enough—"fromage"—you should just go back up there
& tell the girl. I start on Redford's coffee while he looks glumly
at the metal napkin dispenser. Just then, the electric chime
above the door sounds. A man sweeps in & rests
his guitar case on one of the slim café chairs.
His dark hair is arranged in a series of perpetually
breaking wavefronts. A small muscle jumps in his jaw
as he orders a Cinnamon Frenchroll, toasted, with cream cheese.
I lean forward, jabbing Redford with my plastic coffee wand.
Check out that guy over there I say. *Intense.*
Redford shrugs. *I think he's Irish* I say, watching the man bite
into his bagel. The instrument case hovers on the chair edge.
He could have a guitar in there, or else—a sword from the Crusades.
I press my tongue into the square-shaped hole in the lid
of my coffee cup. *Listen* Redford says. *If we're going to be together*
you have to take this. He pushes a small velvet box across the table.
What are you doing? I ask, but Redford doesn't answer.
He just looks down at the table, one hand pressed
to each of his temples. In the box is a square of chocolate
like the top of a signet ring, smooth, but edged

15

in something bright. *It's smoked salt from Wales*, Redford says.
Handmade in limited quantities. I turn the little box
in my hands. The salt sparkles like an arctic church.
I have to blink against it all.

EN ROUTE

Ten miles from Iowa City, Redford pulls over & snaps the dash lights off. *What can you possibly mean* he says, turning *when you ask if I'm sure about you?* He leans into the darkness between us, pulling at the emergency brake with a series of hard clicks. I feel him waiting there across the dark, but I don't know what to say. So I unbuckle my seatbelt, letting the nylon strap tighten from view. I slowly remove my gloves & place them on the dashboard. The cooling engine makes a ticking sound from when Mom & I would wait in empty parking lots while my father was at night school. I would wear pajamas then & eat graham crackers & cold peanut butter in the backseat. Those were hurting times, listening to old songs & watching the orange lights from I-83 sweep down. It was hurting to believe we couldn't sleep in the dark, even if we stayed quiet in the dark, even if we needed to lie down there. The dark had us in it & the dark moaned with the lights of cars, with diamonds coming after us, & after us, the lights were flying. Once, I saw a man. He walked up to the car & tapped a knife against our window. Mom got out, stood in the broken light to scoop coins from her purse & say the names of coins—*a dime, a dime, a dime*—& I thought *how would it be to work in darkness, & who would wait for me in darkness?* I thought *I will make a tent for him.* I make a small tent of my fingertips & look at Redford. His face is a halting city of returns. *What do you think will happen* I say *what will happen?* I listen to the car moving its slow metallic tongue. *What will happen doesn't have to hurt us, ever.* His breath blooms over me, a moth of stillness. *Still, still, still*—I am burning.

THE PROPOSAL

I wake up, & Redford says *Delivered from the tender mouth of sleep at last?*
He drops a kiss on my forehead, then adjusts his cufflinks in the
washstand mirror. *I'll see you soon* he says. I watch him pull a dark suit
coat across his shoulders & slide a folded pair of spectacles into the
breast pocket. Blinking, I start to raise my head above the covers; the
bedroom sharpens with the cedar tang of his cologne. I can't say what
time it is, exactly. On the radio, a little Bach is playing: *Den tod niemand
zwingen kunnt.* I move to the center of the mattress & draw the pale
duvet over me. Snow gathers on the skylight, a flock of bruises. I hear
Redford close the door & the room settles into a parched stillness. *This
is the edge of winter* I think, pushing my wrinkled pajama shirt down. My
tongue is dark with sleep & basking. In the night, I seemed to carry a
straw-colored child through a crumbling rail station, with the dirt-
smoke smell of necks & stained viscose on both of us, & the child
moving its insectile limbs as I hurried. I had a blanket, orange with
brown horses, & I'd covered the child as you would a dish of broth.
With my arms brimming, I couldn't see anymore what I had covered,
& the broken portals of the stationhouse shone blank & cunning. So I
ran, until I stood with one foot on the rim of an open train car & saw
how the floor teemed with belts of sheet metal. It was no place for us. I
folded back the blanket & looked into its robbed center: no child
jackknifed there, no aching made its tilted call. *Kein Unschuld war zu
finden*: In another time, I would have swung for this.

NESTLÉ

I'm washing dishes at the kitchen sink, & Redford
puts his arms around my waist. He says: *I want
to tell you something. You float around my house all day
just like a little cloud of sweetness. That's all.*
He kisses the back of my earlobe, then reaches
over my head to take a Lion bar from the cupboard.
He keeps one hand on my back, & I hear him
opening the candy wrapper with his teeth.
For a moment, his body makes the tilted well
I'm standing in, a slur of tall colors & the soft
press of his palm against the knot
of my apron, & I think of how I would climb
into the middle drawer of my childhood dresser
& balance there, reaching up for the book
called *Rabbit Hotel*. Once, a big square of plywood
broke from its glue & I dropped straight through the drawer.
For a long time, I stayed—not crying, but waist-deep
in the hoop I'd caused & smelling the fresh splinters
which smelled bright & chattered to me like new birds.
Now I turn carefully away from the sink, bestowing
a dollop of pink suds on Redford's cheek. *Aren't you
supposed to say stuff like that while biting a long-stemmed rose?*
Redford smiles over the horizon of his chocolate
& a few suds melt into his shirt collar.
That's for me to know he says. He takes another bite of candy
narrowing his eyes into small, blue pins. Suddenly I'm laughing
without sound, my face a blooming cactus of tears

my soapy arms trailing about his shoulders.
Hold on, hold on says Redford, pulling me.
My hands fill with the darkened
fabric of his shirt; I am rising.

SENSE-CERTAINTY

Do you know says Redford *what I was thinking*
just now? He looks at me, as if through leaves.
I was thinking, now I'm with her. Now her body is under
my hands. You know that feeling of daybreak?
You were stretching away from me, bright. Complete—
like when you wake up with dreams of water still trembling
on you, & you want to pull yourself
down again, like an engine or a flag. That kind.
Redford draws the hem of my T-shirt up & puts
his hand on my belly. *I know you* he says, & smiles
into the room's hush. *When you're not here, I feel you anyway.*
You're on the street, crossing the street. You're going
into a shop with a wooden door shaped like a sun.
I see you drinking from a cup of saffron tea
or eating a slice of white cake.
You have a way of walking out from places.
It's tilted, not in time, as if you made it up.
He slips his hand across my waist, then along
my torso, pressing tightly. *I know the secret shape*
in you. It's in the bone, burning there—
a thing I can't call. Fine-made.
A shape with the sky in it, & so much quiet.
I could drive all my horses through & never reach the end.
But I've been thinking, deciding now—
If I just knew the words to still you down, some sound
to ride by. I'd find a way to keep you with me, then.

If you just asked me to give up my horses
I'd give up my horses.

MARC TRANSIT

Somewhere above Quantico, I leave Redford asleep
with his face curled into the crook of his arm.
I walk into the train bathroom & start unbuttoning my blouse.
In the fluttering dark, in the *shing* of the track
in the wreckage of my skin beneath the rust-starred
mirror, there are no straight lines, & no surfaces to truss.
If you can slide a ballpoint pen under your breast
& the pen stays, it means your tissue is sagging down.
You have to do something.
I touch my fingers to the rim of the sink.
I touch my forehead to the mirror, as if waiting for a circlet.
I say: *You have to do something*.
I open the painted hooks at the back of my bra.
The straps come down.
I take off my bra, I fold it in half, I tuck the straps
& the rigging into the cups. I lean back.
The narrowest part of a woman
is this distance, the band of the body just under
the breastline. I have a body that I flatter with straps.
I have a denim jacket that ends at the tilted
narrows of this cage. At my hips, the cellophane scars
are rising like acanthus, like brittle tongues of ice, like insects
walking on their sutured legs. I walked all day
in the room of pilasters. I lay down for a game.
A man put his hand on my breast. He told me: *You have*
an exciting smell, like the sea. He told me: *Your smell*
is not strong. At the sea, I was twisting

into a rope of sound. I was rising up from a ring of birds.
At the sea, I put my best foot ahead of my next.
Now I let my bra drop onto the floor.
The train shakes over a joint in the tracks
& I raise my arms. Sunlight ranting
down my chest like machines.

QUESTION

Redford asks: *What do you suppose the first*
sound is, after you die?

He turns onto one elbow & looks
down at me.

I don't know I say. *Do you really mean*
right after?

I trace the ribbing on the collar of his T-shirt
with my thumb. I can't count the ribs, but I can
feel them.

Redford says: *I mean right after.*
He closes his hand over mine.

It's very quiet in this room. It feels like
being at the bottom

of a shadow, at the bottom of
a room.

Tell me I say.
I have to stop counting.

Otolaryngology

WHITE

White rises from her nest of tines. Her teeth tall tablets in the precincts of the dark. Cold as airborne, old as basking, loose as dirted screens of salt on salt. White drags her swordwhite self packed down in rice. Touches you between your hanger & your hips, between your tongue & tamp. White, her smell of ash & sour sky, her rasp of baling wire, white. Tonight her mouth, a wolfish star of tamarind. All night her wolfish mouth, against the kitchen of your chest. How white her mouth of wilderness & char. How white her wolfish sleeve of trees, her touch of trees, her tree of broken hair & nails & breath, her broken breath the tree you break yourself against. So white against the solemn trellis of the air. So white the test of air, its solemness, its strike.

THE HUMAN TONGUE SLOWS DOWN
TO SPEAK

Silted slab, gone white with injury
in decorated dark, in budding vault of mayflies

blind & basking, lifts itself:
Is it birch trees again, is it breakfast again

No bowl of branches here, nor light to brood
in shallow pellicles.

The tongue inclines, a-swim with char
& pheasant grease.

Opines:

>*Mother was a sieve.*
>*Father wept.*

>*How will I speak, when all my bones*
>*are hewn from nets I ate*

>*the little birds all from?*

Now, the swollen deck of summer lolls.
The tongue begins & can't begin.

To dock the dawn as it swamps the tonsils—
To catch the blazing protists down.

Such slur of mud in mouth.
Such blackened clang & yards not ringing

in such house.
The tongue stills, lordly.

White root in the vascular dark.
White trumpet in the dark's

low tent.

AFRO

Whereas these strands, well-oiled & diligent in their parts, & appearing in tensile character an iron cloud-net several times the diameter of the head—these strands have I in passing conduct, fidelity, & stewardship, in all protein & mineral accompaniments, in darkness of kerchief & darkness of hands, these have I spirited across the snow & the American seas, from thence to plinths & palettes opportune for discharge of this trust—these strands, which rest in trust to me & which I have dragged a small way into this Country, seeking & halting, desirous to prevent mishap, the undue severance of charge, the tease, the crop & bang, desirous only of those victuals which may furniture my constant guard—whereas for this have I gainsaid the touch of free-booter, the tang of sea-rover & divers others—drinkers, tinkers, kings & clothiers all. These strands, wherein silence bides, close as horses in an afternoon of rain, these ropes which rise against containment & the blur of slang, for these do I come forth in torrents, do I come forth in tenderness & earth do I come forth in rage *for these, for these.*

OR

After Thomas Sayers Ellis

Or oreo, or worse.
Or spork. Or smorgasbord.
Or tender lure of colored blood
or centaur.

Or Moorish curve of orchid.
Or fork-scraped pate, or orphic word.
Or minor saint in darkened
corridor.

Or Overlord of Stars
or what remains of cordwood.
Or touch of orchard wind—
Or taste of swords.

Or path, or means
for dragging ore from earth.
Or earth, where we were built
& bound—

Or elemental source. Or
hopeful spore. Or promontory
light. Or oarsman on the brink
of shore.

Or shorn of slang & char.
Or full of orbits, full of doors

Or drawers of trees & tongues
to claim:

It was like April in Andalucía.
Or, *Chapter One: I am born.*

SAINTS

I have kissed
their wire mouths & trembled

at the taste of window screen & wet
tarnish. I have held

the saint of lightning. Of porches.
I have scratched the dirt

saints & the fever saints that root
beneath my hair.

A fork saint gives me cakebread:
I hunger.

The field saint in my skin
who rakes:

I balm. I slake.

& now I move outward, crossing
the stelled field

where the wheel saint works
his combine.

Turn. Turn. Brink. Turn.
Fast & stormwhite

Through the tumbled
stalks—

Tall saint.
Sword saint.

SECRET NINJA

You thought you saw me!
But you didn't.
I wear black turtlenecks.
Black panties.
Live in a tall cave!

You don't know where my cave is.
But I come out.
Every day!
To buy mustard & relish!
See what—

A man.
Walking away from me.
No good.
Smash him!
With a loud smash!
Smash his metal table and cards.
Good!

Down in my cave.
Put on my Seahawk gear!
Watch *Parade of Homes*.
Watch Ron Popeil put chicken & fishes
& burgers & pork & macaroni in the same
box. Hey! I can sell that

box! At school.
Where I smash the gym teacher in his head!
I don't wear my uniform.
I don't clean my locker.
I don't share my lunch with the athletes.

My lunch—mustard.
Straight from the packet.
No one sits next to me.
Keep working my skills.
Keep circling the word *blood*
in *Macbeth*.

Good.

It takes days.
It takes days.

BITCHFOXLY

Is this he asks *where you keep it this where you keep it this the*
board where you keep it the flitch on the palm where you keep it the rotor
that keeps it the train of the camlet where keeps it is this where you
keep it the druid that keeps it the shoepeg that keeps it the window the
weep in the spine where you keep it is this where you keep it is this
where you keep it is this when you open this open it

LETTER

I wish to express my concern about what's happening. You will say: *what's happening is none of my concern*. Nevertheless, I've just returned from the scene of certain events. Events that by any reasonable standard should inspire grave concern. Try as I may, I can't pretend not to have witnessed what I've witnessed. Try as I may, I can't quiet this concern. It will not go sweet for you, nor drop. My concern is a flare of birdshot in a brake of cedars, which dazzles me from rest. You are the small, dark frill of lichen at the water's brink. I must speak with you. I must come over to you so that I may speak. Hello. Hello, there. Don't you know what's happening? I wish to express my concern. *Such scenes, such scenes as I have lately witnessed*—but this is no way to begin. Let me begin. Let me say: *Together, we must move concernfully from thing to thing*. As light breaks upon the cedars, so the cedars break themselves, and so the wild sounds of birdshot break, break upon the axis of our mutual concern. On this issue we have long said one thing and done another, as if what's happening has nothing needful in it. But certain events will not go sweet for us, nor drop. Now that I'm here with you, speaking with you, at the tender brink of quiet, witness. From here, I inseal you in the wild sound of cedars. For always, I inseal you at the brink of my concern. Come here to me. So comes a lightness through the cedars, once. So our God is a god of this.

CRUSADERS

The note you dropped became a bird.
It sleeps in my chest.
The bird is white.
How fast it dreams.
How slur.
A silence in the canebrake.

When we came to the canebrake.
I tore my yellow coat. You spoke to a bird.
Tall slur
of sunlight on the water's chest.
In dreams
you take my coat into your white

shell mouth. I race among the hard white
stalks of cane, breaking
my feet sharply against their gloss. I dream
a bird
lands on the wooden desk in my chest
to slur

its bones with ink. You slur
above me like white
linen rolling outward from a tea-chest.
Come. We can sleep in the canebrake.
I know a bird
that drops down. Dreams

are falling from its beak, & some dreams
even slur
so that the bird
may stay & speak to both of us, more white
for our time in the canebrake
sleeping chest

to chest.
How the bird trebles in our dreams
of what can break.
Inclining hard into the slur
of small exits. White
houses fold. Each roof a bird

moving in the slur
that cane-stalks make as turning white
we fill with birds—

YOU HAVE MADE A CAREER OF
NOT LISTENING

God has spider skin and lives in secret trees. I have stood beside you, saying
this, as you reach into the cupboard for another stack of dry noodles.
You eat them with the dead still on, with the sticky deadness still on,
because you always throw out the foil package of seasoning. So the
noodle brick just loosens, slowly, in a flat brine of city water, just squats
and spreads in the center of the frying pan like a washed-up boxer or a
stranger's face disappearing into morphine. After the fight the boxer
wraps a towel around his hips and walks into his manager's office. Some
boys wipe fifty bucks' worth of sweat from the ring, then head to the all-
night diner smelling like stacks of thumbs. Meanwhile, dollar bills are
blooming in the stranger's lonely raincoat pocket. It is 5:00 a.m. There
are places you will never go with me, no matter how many times you
ask, or how hard you eat.

ANECDOTE

for PMc

A man is climbing palm trees, cutting down coconuts for everyone.
He puts a plastic straw in the top and lets you drink the milk, which
tastes warm, & the woman, she will not leave me to my own thoughts:

> *I want a coconut. I want a coconut.*
> *I would be happy but I don't have a coconut.*

But I tell her, it's too late, you'll be awake with a bad stomach, let's go
back to the hotel. Only she is saying, no. *I want a coconut*, & now
others have stopped walking to listen. I tell her, let's go back to the
hotel, baby, then tomorrow before it's too dark? Coconut. OK? I have
to lead her away with my hands. In the morning, it is not later than
seven, she puts her pretty tongue into each of my ears to wake me.

> *Well? What about my coconut.*

& I am thinking, shall I kill her now?
Or give her a coconut first?

LOVE POEM

Say *want*. Say *dear*.
Say *A robin sat humming in the deep*
willow. Here is union: two blue eggs
two lights & two hums. In the willow
which hums, say *hum*. Say *willow*
with your thin throat humming. Now, where
is willow? Where *robin* on the light support?
Two quick hums, two quick lights—yes
a braided nest for two, & a branch
for dear robin. Then, humming willow.
Then *egg* & *egg*. Taking bright hold
of the branch. Willow of lungs
afire—

VIRGINIA

Beneath a tender flitch of skin, the grease
ants make & traffic. O brown fliskmahoy
of speed. O limit case. Why linger
at this roadside? Why stretch your bloody ankles
into the sun's mouth? Here, the redstem filaree
spins her basal rosette—your broken hands
catch down in tangles. But don't you smell the wild
bergamot? The tarnished wheel of knapweed
at your crown? How the dirt is rasping
O my trackside love, my age—

SONNET K

Kneel down, river. The river dead with glim.
A dead face parted in the forehead. Having boats.
Myself a kneeler. About to kneel into my head.
At Malaga, before the night boats go. Glim in holes.
Kneel down boats. Night boats parted in the face.
Go down rivers down in holes. Myself a kneeler.
About to kneel before the face. *Maria*.
Golden face. *Maria*. Glim boats go.
Maria. *Maria*. See the river in her holes.
About to kneel into the river. See? In her.
Not circling back, not parting back. About to kneel
into my head. Kneel down. Kneel down. Kneel down
dead with boats. Kneel down and let the dead boats go.
Kneel down the dead face go down kneel down dead I kneel down—

GRISTLE

Uncle tips his plate into the chicken
yard. Chicken War begins

down in the veins & blue leg fat. *Scratch*.
I have a plate.

Scratch. Chickens toss skinny
brown I hold

my plate sogged
with grease & dirty chicken

bones I ate
the yellow meat all from.

Go ahead says Uncle.
Sure don't like to waste that sure

don't like to waste that
sure not

me. Now my plate goes.
Soft & white

over the wire
top lookathem says Uncle lookahow birds

eat up that chicken.
I lookahow birds eat up that

chicken good
God chickens'll eat up that

chicken girl.
Chickens'll eat chicken

girl best
cover up those dirty

legs—

I didn't know infants in arms until

the Italians used it, carrying their babies through the war in a cotton dark of elbows, bombs & pamphlets snowing the marketplace & men pulling tarps over their flats of salt cod. Then I came home & my mother said *your sister was an infant in arms*. But I couldn't think how she belonged in that kind of hurry, trailing cookies over my mother's shoulder & pulling at her wishbone necklace, breaking it. My mother, who wore tennis shoes even when Loch Raven Boulevard iced over & saw possibilities for me as one of Robert Palmer's backup girls, did carry us occasionally but never hurried, snapping half a piece of white gum & asking us did we each want half, too. I haven't had any gum in weeks, nor seen the ground without salt. Winter trash circles the dirty football pitch across the way. Plastic bags, gum wrappers—it doesn't look good. Having once slept on the Vaporetto, all trash smells wet to me, like cheese rinds & old newspapers logged in water. Especially when I fold my elbows under my head. Then, the water & trash split into gasoline colors, the peanut shells move too lightly around the boat. What a smell. I can't bring it up in Baltimore—we don't eat the same things here, we have highways, it's different.

NEGATION

Sometimes I make an *X* of it.
The bearded saint asleep in his muddy Peterbilt.
The teens drinking cola in riot gear above a gone city.
I make decisions. I take my *X*-pencil & slick it
over whole traincars & kitchens, & plastic
dumpsters filled with cake frosting. I hear the *whump* of things
going out of focus. & yes—I hear the saint
call out & tumble from his yellow rig. I see the iron sky burn
& hatch with *X*s. The teens knuckle into
their dogs' kerchiefs to hold them back. The
dogs are eating asphalt, the dogs want to break
themselves, the dogs shake, they wheedle,
they scrap for earthly brightnesses,
for concrete trestles edged with ice, for the broken
haunch of winter in their breath
for brown dials of blood, the pointed ribs of
the dogs quicken. Now, I am busy.
Now, I hear: *Who is she?*

O LORD

I lift my heart from its brown

clock & shake
long enough to catch the sad loose

switch in it.
Slow thing I say tender. *I'll miss*

tapping in the fine broke
days.

Jingle days—
My heart would mark in bird

sound. A silver *thrum* now hushed.
Hush—

This keeping, unless you *stir*
my heart O Lord

today. Unless you lift me up & tap
just where. Two taps

may sound
through to the metal—

—Through—
—*Through*—

CROSSING

This daily cloud is courtesy & not a road.
So I tell you, rosin up. For surely you know
not the audit, nor the time of setting forth.
I tell you, put your feet in the correct prints.
Press your knees against the mountain, or against
your cabin door & you will hold. Take no
moving walkways from here, nor bundle your hair
in heavy scarves. Take no farthing with you, no
algebraic X. Leave your animals to chew their tethers.
Kneel down. In the quiet plank of midnight, speak
not of thunderheads nor of the web that drags
its spokes in milk. Take not your women
by the neck. Take not yourself
from me.

Valentine

VALENTINE

I hope your father built a treehouse in the soft
shade below the creek. I hope it glimmered there, between two
poplars. I hope you stood at your mother's sleeve
while she fixed madeleines for breakfast. It was Easter.
All six of your aunts adored you. For your country project
you picked Tunisia because of its peanut shape.
Which was your first rock show?
Mine was Milli Vanilli. I hope you licked the ends of your colored
pencils. Also, that you carried a Trapper Keeper. The first time a girl
touched you, I hope you had graham crumbs on your mouth. I hope
she wore her brother's hunting coat, latchless.

Do you also dislike beets? I hope so. I hope you're
reading all the classics, like *Moby Dick*. When the preacher
climbs the ladder made of ropes? That's the best. I did that
once, at an amusement park. I believe the stars get brighter
when it's cold. Do you like riding in convertibles? I like
riding in convertibles. I like how sunflowers turn themselves
into big radios. I used to live where canola oil's from. I used
to eat fried zucchini flowers and tomato salad. What do you
like for breakfast? Do you listen to BBC News? When you make
someone a sandwich, I hope you trim the casings from each
slice of salami. No one likes to eat those.

I try to think of what you'll need from Walgreens.
Maybe you've got contacts. In which case, you can just use
my solution. What diseases run in your family? Will we have to worry

about strokes? I'll probably live to be quite old. I hope you'll let me
lay out your pajamas. Not every day, but sometimes.
Will you eat bran patties
for breakfast then? What about those S-cookies? Those come from Sicily.
I've seen them in the shops. I've seen women in gold slingbacks
on the bus. That's OK, but I hope we'll have our own car. I know a church
with a dark ceiling. The Normans built it. It's sad until you drop coins
into this special lamp: *clink*, *clink*. After that, it's different, see.

VALENTINE

Suppose it was a cold throwdown for my affection.
Who would win, Jack White or Jack Black?

You have to think in three dimensions here:
Jack White, Jack Black, & one acoustic guitar.

I'm the fourth dimension in a yellow wig & small purse.
OK, let's have a ref.

I choose Senator Patrick Leahy, Democrat, of Vermont.
We all gather at the bar: *Hi, Ref.*
We all get free No. 2 pencils from Vermont.
Vermont is rad.

Then we see a mini throwing-star. It's zipping over us.
It's Jack Black's.

Intense I say. Jack White opens his shirt. He takes out
some kind of raptor. *This is totally poisonous* he tells me.
Cool I tell him.

It'd be pretty cool to win this fight for you.
I mean, throwdown he says.

The poisonous raptor spits onto the floor.
Jack White isn't hot, exactly.

Another mini throwing-star goes by.
I decide to stand behind the bar.

Bartender says: *Little darlin' that is some doggone wig.*
Come on & get you some Grainbelt.

We drink our Grainbelts.
We watch the raptor dig a hole in Jack Black's neck.

Now he's stacking mini throwing-stars inside.
Bartender says: *Moves secretary-like.*

Sure does I say. I bet you can't speak too well
with a neck full of blades.
I'm not sure, but I'm pretty sure.

Once, I saw the moon.

VALENTINE

All the good ones are in the war.
—Grandma

Maybe you *were* in the war, all this time.
For surely you did not attend my high school.

Nor did you ever climb the white dogwood tree
under my window in Baltimore.

You weren't in the ice cream truck that stopped.
Or in the ice cream truck that didn't.

You weren't in the quarry.
You weren't in the whole nation of Switzerland.

You didn't give me penicillin in an eyedropper
when I had scarlet fever that time.

You didn't tell me I was delicate.
Or pick me up from work in your Escalade.

You weren't in my laundry. Or in the tiny moustache
of that Frenchman I frenched.

Perhaps you were in the war then?
Or: when I walked by, you'd just taken this huge bite

of peanut butter sandwich?
Maybe you were wearing a T-shirt that read: *Official Pussy Inspector*.

So, you're an Official Pussy Inspector.
Or: you lived before the time of Christ.

What if you got killed by lions in the gladiator ring?
What if you were allergic to sand?

Your mother might have dug your cradle in the forest floor.
And maybe you grew down, into the clay.

Your skin might be the color of rain, then.
Eyes like trees.

Perhaps you're walking to the center of the earth right now.
Then up, to catch the moon by her arms.

Sometimes you feel as close to me as the river
I tremble across.

Is it you who fills the evening pines with light?
I'd like to find you.

I'd like to win a Fulbright to your tilted acreage
in outer space, where you milk

the tears of horses.
Then, I'd let you push my hair into a crown.

I'd let you lift me over.
Then, in shadows.

VALENTINE

Once, I was your precious lintel.
Your roof, your floor, your deck of gingerbread.

You said: *For what is love, my darling, but a bower*
built from Pop Tarts?

A Pop Tart but a torso, frostified with pain?
& pain—what is that, but sprinkles?

You opened your hands, blinking:
O lintel.

Then, some steel guitar.
The leggy *hellothere* of crickets.

I removed my watch & hatpin.
Boarded your bed & sailed:

> *Camphor wood—*
> *—Pergola*
> *Star anise—*

On the other side, a supper.
Plates of sliced duck breast, purée of white bean.

We drank broth from empty oyster shells & smoked
under the moon-colored pines.

Hours passed & circled us.
A tree lifted, black on less black.

You covered me with a quilt of navy percale.
Stood, smiling.

Hellothere you said *& welcome, from the wide world.*

How an oar of wind pulled through me, then.
I became as large as doors & thresholds

& felt, & felt
against your tenderness

a sea—

VALENTINE

Sorry, but I just don't love you
more than Darwinism.

More than: *Farmers take their animals to feed*
upon the alpine balds.

I don't love you more than this cheese slice
which tastes of Swiss feet.

I don't love you more than falling off the
button lift, or haul lines,

or deciding whether peanut M&Ms are treats
or snacks.

I don't love you more than old darknesses
and sipping from thimbles.

I just don't love you.
I just don't love you more than pizza.

Or the final scenes of *Clue.*
Or colored chalk.
Or what Clive Owen's jaws are made out of.

I don't love you more than the social imagination.
Or more than NPR on Sunday.

Or my own face, glyphed
with tulip pollen.

I don't love you more than the word *classic*.
Or my afro.
Or this badass wrestling singlet.

No. But you're better off.
I'd only cause you grief, in time.

Abandon you for someone jazzy, more hirsute—
Probably. I guess.

I mean, *maybe* if you stepped into the singlet right now.
Theoretically. Just to see.

Wait— Wait—
(...)

Nope.

VALENTINE

Today I met my favorite butcher again.
He walked right up to me & asked:

What can I get for you today?
Well— I said. I wanted the 85% lean beef.

How about the 85 beef I said.
I mean, lean I said.

My butcher wrapped the beef in white paper.
Touch under a pound he smiled.

I made tacos.
It was the perfect amount of 85% lean beef.

I thought: *Food is ingenious.*
Way ingenious.

Because:
      Ordering food
      is really ordering *some of the food.*

      Not *any* food.
      Just this one food, thanks.

But:

        You can't order *some of the love.*
        It's not scientific.

        So you get the wrong love.
        Or you get the wrong amount.

        Chrysler Building Love when you wanted Dinner Roll Love.
        Switchgrass Love instead of Foghorn Love.

        Like, I've had:
                Canyoneering Love
                Espresso Love
                Removable T-Top Love
        None of which I ordered.

But, OK:

Once, I took the ferry to Capri, where
I ordered a plate of *rigatoni all'arrabbiata.*

I was alone.
I was wearing a black leather jacket.

I'll have some of the rigatoni all'arrabbiata I said.
I gave a mystical half-smile.

There were sailboats in the ocean that day.
There was a Circle Island Tour.

What'll it be like, buying a ticket? I thought.
I liked the word *ticket* very much.

I liked how my chair slanted.
No one sat with me, except a glass carafe.

I felt fine, actually.

Then my rigatoni came.
There were these big onions in it, & ham cubes.

The island hates me I thought.
It wants me to eat these ugly onions & ham.

I endured a bite.
Then, another.

Then, I said: *I didn't order some of the foods which
are in some of my rigatoni.*

The waiter said: *Which foods?*
I said: *Some of the onions & ham, please.*

He said: *But you are American, yes?*
Americans eat surely of the ham, & onion.

I said: *Yes, but this is not what I ordered.*
He said: *We gave of your order. Then, also, we gave
of your wish.*

69

I pointed to the carafe: *Does it also wish of onions?*
I said *This onion, what does it wish?*

To meet Americans? I said.
I quickly pointed to my heart.

To meet me? An American?
The waiter's eyes swept down.

I believe this onion is American he said.
I kept pointing.

VALENTINE

In Chicago, I hooked up with a certified chef.
All I desired was ruthlessness, & Benito

worked at Soldier Field, filling steam-trays
with chicken & legumes. His steam-trays occupied

the finest of skyboxes. In a way, they were sky trays
& Benito, a certified sky chef.

He'd framed his skills around a single dish:
Green beans amandine.

Goes with chicken, goes with trout. He rested
a decisive hand on my knee.

Benito's nails were clean & pink as cutting boards.
In the past half-hour, he'd uttered

more than seventeen declarative sentences.
Take me someplace fine I told him.

I stood up, brushing my palms across the plastic
rigging of his Bears cap.

We went to my house.
What's this doing in your sink? Benito asked.

It was the Booth edition of Shakespeare's Sonnets.
I'd left it under a medium-slow faucet all night.

That's my homework I said. *I've got to open up
the text some.*

The metal sink brimmed with pages.
I hoisted myself onto the butcher-block island.

*If you check the fridge, I think there's a bag
of green beans.*

Benito held the little ziploc.
Where am I supposed to wash these?

I motioned to the sink, but Benito shook his head.
Not with all that Shakespeare.

Fine. I grabbed a colander from the overhead
rack & jumped down.

But you don't know what you're missing here I said.
I mean, Booth's notes are just super.

I dragged my colander across the floating skin
of paper.

Talk about the Rolls Royce of notes I said.
I filled a large juice glass with soggy sheets.

Benito spoke quietly. *Amandine is strictly skybox.*
He lifted a mass of beans & sighed. *Are we really doing this?*

Why not? I said. *Sink's fine now.* With my tongue, I lifted
the tab on a tiny can of smoked almonds.

Stop doing that Benito said, trembling back.
That isn't right.

He hurried over to his fleece & put it on.
Thou art the grave I grinned across the kitchen.

I swam my hands up.

VALENTINE

I build you from a crust of glass.
I build you.

From frost, from cinnamon
I build you.

From the wood of the pear tree
From horses on the covered bridge

From fennel soap & thyme
I build you.

I build you from glades.
I build you from scree.
I build you from soft shells of light.

I build you from the twelve
stoneflies I captured in a foil drinking cone.

From the Gunpowder River I build you.
From willow trees, from canoes filled with snow.
From the crown of trees, from the rag & crown of trees
I build you.

From the wideness
From the white & wondering places

From towers, from stones
From the dandelions there, from the towers there
From the broken sky above the towers, from the stripe of sky
From the *yes* of sky

From a time of *yes* & no water
From spider crabs, from a smack of thirst
From salt-starred floorboards & from catching

I build you.
I build you.

From touching, from falling, I build you.
From afternoons of sleep, from sleeping through rains
From lightning in the far valleys, from your belt on the chair
From houses, from crags, from fields.

From these, I build you.
I build you.

From this trench, I build you.
I build you.

From this trench of light, I build you.
I build you, light.

O light
O light
O light

I build you here, O light.
From the trenches, from the wild depths
From my own from

my wild from my taken
rib—

VALENTINE

Today I got rejected from the Bible.
They sent a special envelope, which turned to palm ash

when I opened it. A whiff of frankincense floated down
from the wreckage, & a girl's voice said:

Thanks for the look.

We've no room at present, but
your poems are stylish & convincing.

We hope you'll try us again.
Best, Agnes

Stylish? Convincing? Sounds pretty nice.
But riddle me this—*Agnes*:

Why. Does this always. Happen.

Just tell me—since you're *so* smart.
OK?

You probably don't *need* that Bible gig—
What with your solid gold Camaro & your hunting dogs.

But me, Agnes? I'm not like you.
I can't afford to lick ambergris off my servants' bellies all day.

I *do* need the Bible.

It's a personal need, Agnes.
You've placed so much of my friends' work.

Take the Pentateuch.
You've tucked *The Book of Nico* right there, between

Leviticus & Numbers. Which is fine, OK, but did he really have
to have his own book?

Agnes, I'm asking.

I know you're jousting pink unicorns right now.
You've got a spray-tan scheduled.

Tonight, no doubt you'll sip lime cocktails
in a jacuzzi brimming

with my ex-boyfriends. I do hope you have
a droll & savvy time together.

I'll be here. Silently heating up some pizza rolls.
Then I'll use the computer.

Not to write poems, you understand.
Just—touching the keys.

It's not how anyone should
get healthy, especially not me.

But there's a darkness in that
clicking sound, a bridge so black

I can't get over—

VALENTINE

Once, I wrote a poem
in the manner of Donald Justice's "Twenty Questions."

Except mine was called "Twenty Mobster Questions."
My poem went like this:

> *So you're a wiseguy now?*
> *I said, you think you're a wiseguy?*

It took hours. Afterward, I said:
Smooth work, Vitamin K. You've done it again.

But then I realized:

> *I said, you think you're a wiseguy* is not
> a question; it's a declarative sentence.

So I'd already messed up the piece.
Donald Justice, man.

I'll never beat him on the terrain of grammar.
Or: elegance.

I have to accept this.

But writing about mobsters did make me feel more
Italian for a while.

Which is nice, right?
Of course, my relatives aren't in the Mob.

We don't keep those kinds of secrets, & we don't
talk in question form.

We just yell.
It's because we don't like each other enough

to get rhetorical. Growing up, I didn't know
milk or *cottonwood tree* but I could say

May you shit an orb of fire from your diseased asshole
in pristine dialect.

Who else has that going for them?

This guy I loved—he said
he couldn't see himself with a Mediterranean-style wife.

My whole family's Anglo he joked. *I can't be the only one
whose kids have too much hair.*

I didn't reveal my love for him then.
But I felt sad anyway.

I've never thought of how my kids will look.
They probably *will* have lots of hair.

But that's OK—
I'll comb it for them.

We'll have a dessert party, & the elderly will say:
Look at the beautiful curls on those babies.

I'll gather my hands around my babies' heads.
I'll let the moment go.

Most people can't love you
unless you remind them of someone else.

You have to bring them close to you.
You have to reach.

When I'm reaching for someone, I feel
light & fast enough

to sprint for miles over the broken, empty
air between us.

I don't want to hurt anyone.
Come in.

Let me show you what I made.
Right now, I'm shaking this powdered sugar

over a fresh crostata for you.
I'm putting on my reddest dress, with the *V*

in the back. I'm sweeping an armful of candles
from room to room.

This is my house.

These are my towels & my maps.
This is how to say *towel* in my house:

> *Are you a wiseguy? Here's a towel.*
> *So you think you're a wiseguy? Here.*

Here's my arm, reaching over you.
It's just an arm.

What's not to like about it?
I'll tell you what I wish.

NOTES

"The Proposal": The German lines are from Verse 2 of "Christ lag in Todesbanden (Christ lay in the bonds of death)," a cantata by J. S. Bach.

"The Human Tongue Slows Down to Speak": The title is from a medical paper submitted to *The Annals of Otology, Rhinology, and Laryngology*.

"Or": After the poem "Or," by Thomas Sayers Ellis. The first line is from that poem. In the final couplet, the first italicized line is from the journals of Christopher Columbus as quoted in William Carlos Williams' *In the American Grain*. The second italicized line is from Dickens.

Photo by Rolex. Tomas Bertelsen

THE AUTHOR

Kiki Petrosino was born in Baltimore and received her BA from the University of Virginia. She spent two years in Switzerland teaching English and Italian at a private school, after which she earned graduate degrees from both the University of Chicago and the Iowa Writers' Workshop. Her poem, "You Have Made a Career of Not Listening," was featured in the anthology *Best New Poets 2006* (Samovar Press), and other poems have appeared in *FENCE, The Iowa Review, Forklift, Ohio*, and elsewhere. She lives in Iowa City.